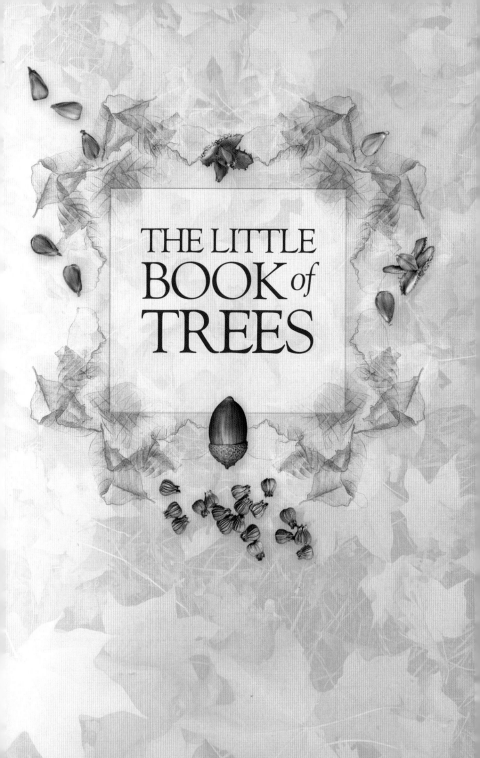

THE LITTLE
BOOK of
TREES

First published in 2019 by Fine Feather Press Limited
The Coach House, Elstead Road, Farnham, Surrey GU10 1JE

2 4 6 8 10 9 7 5 3 1

A CIP catalogue record is available from the British Library

ISBN: 978-1-908489-38-8
Printed in China

www.finefeatherpress.com

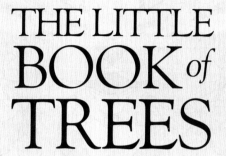

THE LITTLE
BOOK *of*
TREES

A NEW WORLD
TO DISCOVER

Consultant: Dr Gabriel Hemery

CONTENTS

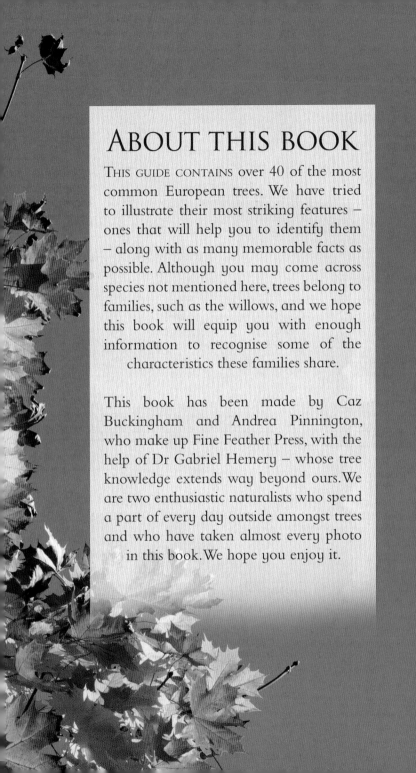

ABOUT THIS BOOK

THIS GUIDE CONTAINS over 40 of the most common European trees. We have tried to illustrate their most striking features – ones that will help you to identify them – along with as many memorable facts as possible. Although you may come across species not mentioned here, trees belong to families, such as the willows, and we hope this book will equip you with enough information to recognise some of the characteristics these families share.

This book has been made by Caz Buckingham and Andrea Pinnington, who make up Fine Feather Press, with the help of Dr Gabriel Hemery – whose tree knowledge extends way beyond ours. We are two enthusiastic naturalists who spend a part of every day outside amongst trees and who have taken almost every photo in this book. We hope you enjoy it.

ALDER
Alnus glutinosa

THE COMMON ALDER is usually found in boggy ground and along riversides. It is a key species in many ways, not least for the food and shelter it provides for animals. The seed is vital for birds such as redpolls, siskins and goldfinches; the roots make perfect nest sites for otters; and many insects such as the chequered skipper butterfly feed and breed within its reach.

Out of sight, the alder's weblike roots help to stabilise riverbanks. They also have bacteria-filled nodules on them which soak up nitrogen from the air, passing it back into the tree and the soil.

LEAVES

These are thick and round, often with a small notch at the end. The alder gives no showy autumn display, for the leaves keep their dark green colour until they fall.

FLOWERS

Male catkins are purple at first, giving the tree a late winter glow. These open to yellow, while the female catkins are small and red. Fruits in the form of woody cones stay on the tree in winter, making alders easy to identify.

WOOD

Not surprisingly for a riverside plant, alder doesn't mind getting repeatedly wet and dry, which made it ideal for bridge supports before the invention of concrete. When alive, alder wood is white, but once it has been cut and exposed to air it becomes an orangy-red colour as shown below.

FACTFILE

HABITAT: Damp
ground and riversides
SIZE: Up to 28 m
FLOWERS: Mar to Apr
HABIT: Conical, often
with several trunks
TYPE: Deciduous
BURNS: Quickly

FACTFILE
HABITAT: Pretty much everywhere • SIZE: 30 to 40 m
FLOWERS: Apr to May • HABIT: Slender with a large,
spreading crown • TYPE: Deciduous • BURNS: Well

ASH

Fraxinus excelsior

IF YOU LOOK UP into an ash, you will be able see the sky. Its light, open canopy allows flowers such as bluebells and wild garlic to flourish underneath. Ash thrives in damp, well-drained soil where its roots hungrily search out nutrients. Its leaves are among the last to open in spring and the first to fall in autumn.

Ash wood is light-coloured and incredibly tough and used to be popular for making tool handles. Recently, ash trees have come under severe attack from ash die-back disease caused by a fungus and few trees are likely to remain unaffected.

BUDS

It is easy to identify an ash tree in winter by its rounded black buds. If you think of ash being sooty, this can make identification easier.

KEYS

The winged keys, which hang in bunches, are a type of fruit known as samara. There is a twist in the samara's wing, which means it spins as it falls, helping to carry it away to grow elsewhere.

WILDLIFE

The importance of ash to wildlife is huge. Nuthatches, owls and woodpeckers use holes in ash trees to make their nests; bats use cracks and cavities for roosting sites; while scores of other birds, insects, mosses, lichens and fungi rely on ash trees and their surroundings.

BUD GALLERY

IT SEEMS OBVIOUS to identify a tree by its leaves, but the buds can be just as distinctive. Look out for how the buds are arranged on the twig – whether opposite, alternating or clumped – their colour, their texture and also how they lie. Some buds nestle in close to the twig while others stick out sideways.

ASH

BEECH

SILVER BIRCH

BLACK POPLAR

HAWTHORN

HAZEL

HORNBEAM

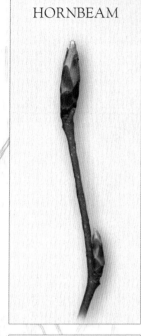

HORSE CHESTNUT

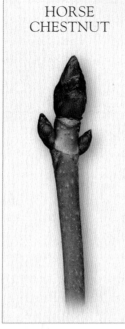

PEDUNCULATE OAK

GOAT WILLOW

SWEET CHESTNUT

SYCAMORE

FACTFILE

HABITAT: Woodland
clearings, scrubland
SIZE: Up to 30 m
FLOWERS: Mar
HABIT: Slender with
few lower branches
TYPE: Deciduous
BURNS: Poorly

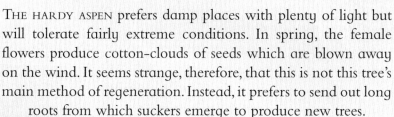

ASPEN

Populus tremula

THE HARDY ASPEN prefers damp places with plenty of light but will tolerate fairly extreme conditions. In spring, the female flowers produce cotton-clouds of seeds which are blown away on the wind. It seems strange, therefore, that this is not this tree's main method of regeneration. Instead, it prefers to send out long roots from which suckers emerge to produce new trees.

In North America, a grove of quaking aspens (closely related to this species) called Pando is over 80,000 years old and consists of over 40,000 identical trees sprouting from the same root system.

BARK AND WOOD

When young, the aspen has smooth, creamy coloured bark, but as the tree ages small black diamonds appear, as you can see below. The wood is extremely light and was commonly used for making arrows, matches and paper.

LEAF NOISE

Young aspen leaves are a bronze colour, but in the autumn they turn a striking yellow. One of the most distinctive things about the aspen is the sound of its leaves fluttering and rustling in the wind. It is easy to see that the leaves have long stalks and a closer look will reveal them to be unusually flat. This causes the leaves to move far more rapidly and frequently than those on other trees, even other members of the poplar family.

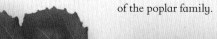

Beech

Fagus sylvatica

TALL, ELEGANT, SUPREME TREE or competitive forest bully? Given the right conditions – not too dry, not too wet, not too hot, not too cold – this mighty tree would push out all others in the struggle to survive. Its graceful branches rise up, reaching out to let their leaves gobble up light in order to make food.

There is very little sunlight left to penetrate the dense canopy once the leaves have unfurled, and few plants are able to grow in this dark understory world. As well as light, the beech needs huge amounts of water – about 130 gallons a day.

MAST YEARS

It may take 80 years before a beech tree produces seeds, commonly known as beechnuts or beechmast. These are housed in spiky four-pronged cases with around 30,000 beechmast being produced in a single season.

The beech does not produce seeds every year. Mast years, as they are known, may be only every five years. At these times, animals such as deer, boar, badgers, mice and squirrels gorge on them, while in the following barren years their numbers dwindle.

USES

Beech timber is strong and easy to work with, and is used to make furniture such as chairs and chests. Strips of bark were once a popular writing material and our word "book" comes from "boc", an Anglo-Saxon word for beech.

FACTFILE
HABITAT: Woods, parks, gardens • SIZE: Up to 40 m
FLOWERS: Apr to May • HABIT: Wide crown, low branches
TYPE: Deciduous • BURNS: Well

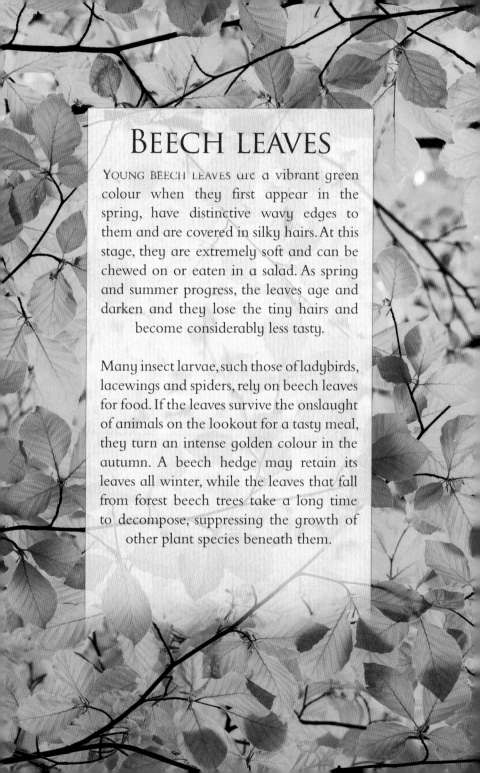

BEECH LEAVES

YOUNG BEECH LEAVES are a vibrant green colour when they first appear in the spring, have distinctive wavy edges to them and are covered in silky hairs. At this stage, they are extremely soft and can be chewed on or eaten in a salad. As spring and summer progress, the leaves age and darken and they lose the tiny hairs and become considerably less tasty.

Many insect larvae, such those of ladybirds, lacewings and spiders, rely on beech leaves for food. If the leaves survive the onslaught of animals on the lookout for a tasty meal, they turn an intense golden colour in the autumn. A beech hedge may retain its leaves all winter, while the leaves that fall from forest beech trees take a long time to decompose, suppressing the growth of other plant species beneath them.

BLACK LOCUST
Robinia pseudoacacia

TRYING TO FIND THIS tree in reference books can be tricky as it may be listed as false acacia, robinia or just locust tree. Originally from North America, it is now widespread throughout Europe, where it prefers warm, dry conditions. It tends to reproduce by sending out root suckers – a system that is so successful that in many places it is considered to be a weed.

Look out for the distinctive deep grey grooves in the bark of older black locust trees. The wood is extremely hard and doesn't rot easily, making it popular for making fence posts and furniture.

FLOWERS

The tree flowers in late spring when dreamily scented long clusters of flowers hang down. Bees that gather the pollen produce the popular acacia honey.

TREE DEFENCES

Two sharp thorns lie at the base of each leaf to deter hungry animals. These may not exist on older trees because once established they do not need to defend themselves from attack.

PODS

The flowers develop into long brown pods. The seeds inside ripen in late autumn, though the pods stay on the branches until spring. The leaves and bark are poisonous, especially to horses, though squirrels feed on the seeds.

FACTFILE
HABITAT: Parks, gardens, roadsides
SIZE: Up to 30 m
FLOWERS: May to June
HABIT: Fast-growing with open canopy
TYPE: Deciduous
BURNS: Slowly

BLACK MULBERRY
Morus nigra

THERE ARE THREE TYPES of mulberry tree – black, white and red. Silkworms feed on the leaves of white mulberry trees while the black species is popularly grown for its fruit. Brave are the mulberry-eaters, for the fruit is quick to stain and spoil which is why it is rarely grown commercially.

The branches and trunk of the black mulberry are often twisted and gnarled and the leaves are late to open. This has earned it the name "Wise Tree", for by the time its leaves appear the danger of frost is thought to have passed.

HEALTH PROPERTIES
Packed with fibre and nutrients, all parts of the mulberry tree can be used medicinally. The leaves are said to strengthen the liver and lungs, while the fruit aid digestion, improve the circulation and slow down the aging process!

FLOWERS
Looking like bundles of tiny maggots, the female flowerheads are about half the size of the male ones. The flowers are pollinated via the wind and slowly form clusters of sweet fruit, which are pale at first before ripening to purple or black.

LEAVES
With ragged edges and a heart-shaped base, the black mulberry leaf is easy to recognise. In autumn, the leaves turn a glorious yellow colour.

FACTFILE
HABITAT: Gardens, parks
SIZE: Up to 12 m
FLOWERS: May to June
HABIT: Domed canopy,
often with twisted,
leaning or split trunks
TYPE: Deciduous
BURNS: Well when dry

LEAF GALLERY

EUROPE IS A LARGE geographical area – ranging from sea level to high mountains – where temperatures vary with the seasons. The forests here contain both coniferous and deciduous trees, and the shape and texture of their leaves are like a set of clues revealing how each tree adapts to survive in different conditions.

CONIFERS

Conifers have tough, thin leaves which are good at conserving moisture, last longer and can tolerate extreme weather conditions. Most conifers have either needles or scales, and are usually evergreen.

GRAND FIR
Needles inserted singly

SCOTS PINE
Needles in bunches

WESTERN RED CEDAR
Scale-like leaves

BROADLEAF TREES

Most deciduous trees have large, flat leaves which fall as the weather gets colder. This lets trees conserve their energy, ready to produce leaves again when it warms up.

COPPER BEECH
Simple leaf on a stem

ROWAN
Leaflets joined to a stem at many points

HORSE CHESTNUT
Leaflets joined to a stem at one point

24

WHITE WILLOW
Long, thin leaf

BOX
Oval leaf

LIME
Heart-shaped leaf

DOGWOOD
Smooth leaf edge

SILVER BIRCH
Toothed leaf edge

HAWTHORN
Lobed leaf edge

HOLM OAK
Short-stalked leaf

GINKGO
Long-stalked leaf

ASPEN
Flat-stalked leaf

GOAT WILLOW
Alternate leaves on a
single stem

ASH
Opposite leaves on a
single stem

MIMOSA
Many leaflets

FACTFILE
HABITAT: Cities, parks
and damp ground
SIZE: Up to 30 m
FLOWERS: Mar to Apr
HABIT: Upright with
rounded outline
TYPE: Deciduous
BURNS: Quickly

BLACK POPLAR
Populus nigra

THIS BOOK FEATURES THREE species of poplar – the black and the Lombardy poplars and the aspen. They are all fast-growing trees, cultivated for furniture, musical instruments, building materials and matches. The Romans planted them around public forums – hence the name *populus*, which means people in Latin.

The black poplar is found throughout Europe, but its numbers are rapidly dwindling and it is becoming one of our rarest trees. Its decline is due to a loss of the floodplain habitat it favours and the fact that it is quick to cross with other poplar species.

WILDLIFE

The black poplar is vulnerable to attack by a number of leaf-eating caterpillars, including this poplar hawk-moth. It lays its eggs on the undersides of the leaves, which the larvae then happily gorge on when they hatch out.

A CLOSER LOOK

The long green female catkins appear on the tree in April. Once pollinated, they form fruit capsules which burst open when ripe to release fluffy white seeds, sometimes referred to as poplar snow. The fluff is used in North America for insulation and as stuffing for pillows, giving the tree its nickname of cottonwood.

The name black poplar is due to the tree's dark, lined bark which is often gnarled and knobbly.

BLACKTHORN
Prunus spinosa

WHEN WINTER SHOWS no other sign of ending, along comes the blossom from the blackthorn tree. A warm February may see the first buds burst open and by March many hedgerows are festooned with its bright white flowers. Once you know this to be blackthorn, you will realise just how common it is.

Wildlife depends on all parts of this tree: the early flowers are a vital source of nectar for bumblebees; many caterpillars feed on the leaves; birds nest among its dense branches; and the great grey shrike or butcherbird hangs its prey on the sharp thorns.

ITS MANY USES

Not only is this tree important to wildlife; humans too have depended on it over the centuries. The wood is extremely hard and was valued as such for crafting walking sticks, clubs and agricultural tools, and when tea was an expensive commodity, blackthorn leaves were used instead. Sloe berries are often gathered after the first frosts and infused in gin to make a syrupy liqueur.

HEDGEROWS

What better plant to use as a barrier for keeping livestock contained than one with savage spines and tangled growth? Beware when picking sloes, for splinters from the thorns can hurt and may get infected.

FACTFILE
HABITAT: Hedges
and thickets
SIZE: Up to 6 m
FLOWERS: Mar
HABIT: More small
woody plant than tree
TYPE: Deciduous
BURNS: Slowly & well

TREE FLOWERS

THIS TWIG FROM A MANNA ASH — an ornamental tree sometimes just called the flowering ash — bears a profusion of creamy-white flowers. The strong scent is designed to attract insects so that they will carry pollen between the male and female parts of the tree's flowers so that the fruit can then form.

All trees have flower-like structures which in conifers develop into cones and in other trees into fruit. The word blossom applies to the flowering displays of stone-fruit trees such as cherries, plums and peaches, and also commonly refers to the similarly showy displays of many types of trees.

FACTFILE
HABITAT: Parks, gardens
and chalk hillsides
SIZE: Up to 6 m
FLOWERS: Apr to May
HABIT: Bush, small tree
TYPE: Evergreen
BURNS: Too valuable
to burn!

Box
Buxus sempervirens

BRUSHING YOUR HAND through box releases a distinctive smell which some people love and others liken to cat pee. Despite the smell, it is a popular garden shrub owing to its glossy evergreen foliage. In the United Kingdom, it is rarely seen in any quantity in woodlands save at a few sites in southern England.

Boxwood is hard and yellow, has a fine grain and, unlike most wood, is denser than water. It is still crafted, as it was in the past, into decorative boxes, printing blocks and musical instruments, though today cheaper materials are more frequently used.

FLOWERS

Box does not produce the most obvious flowers, in fact although creamy yellow they are small and nestle into the base of the leaves, making them quite hard to see.

TOPIARY

Few plants beat box for its ability to be shaped into interesting designs, for the small glossy leaves withstand close pruning. This art is called topiary, from the Latin *topia opera* meaning fancy gardening.

PESTS

Box is incredibly slow-growing so it is tragic when diseases or pests attack it. In recent years, the caterpillars of the deceptively pretty box tree moth have decimated swathes of box throughout Europe. Box blight disease is another major problem, caused by a fungus.

FACTFILE
HABITAT: Large parks and gardens
SIZE: Up to 40 m
FLOWERS: Autumn
HABIT: Tall with wide sweeping branches
TYPE: Evergreen
BURNS: Explosively

CEDAR OF LEBANON
Cedrus libani

FEW TREES CAN BE as majestic as the cedar of Lebanon. It adds a grandeur to any scene and was popularly planted in many stately homes and parks from the 18th century onwards. It is one of the easiest trees to identify with its bright green foliage and long spreading branches, which start close to the ground where its thick trunk begins to divide.

Cedar resin was used by Ancient Egyptians for embalming dead bodies, and great forests of cedars were destroyed around the Mediterranean in order to build temples, palaces and boats.

NEEDLES AND CONES

Cedars have short, narrow needles grouped in bunches which stay on the tree for three to six years. The female cones sit upright on the branch and have a distinctive barrel shape.

BARK

The bark of the cedar of Lebanon is a dark greyish-brown colour and becomes deeply ridged as the tree ages. It produces a fragrant resin which, along with other parts of the tree, is aromatic and acts as an insect repellent.

FUNGI

Despite the fact that cedar sap wards off most insects, it does not protect the tree from certain fungi. One such organism called honey fungus feeds off trees like this cedar, often until they die.

CONIFEROUS FORESTS

A WALK THROUGH a coniferous forest can be an eerily quiet experience. There is a reason for this. Conifers are evergreen trees, such as pines, firs and spruces, specially adapted to life in areas with poor soil and harsh weather conditions, where most broadleaf trees would struggle to survive. Few other plants can tolerate it here either, so there is often little in the way of understory vegetation, and without this to feed on there are not many animals. Hence the silence.

Any sound is dampened yet further by the needles that cover the forest floor, for even though conifers tend to keep their thin leaves for several years, they do finally fall.

Coniferous forests are an important source of timber for making paper and for use in the building industry and, like all trees, conifers store the carbon we breathe out.

CORSICAN PINE
Pinus nigra subsp. *salzmannii*

A WALK THROUGH A Corsican pine plantation is like being on holiday in the Mediterranean – which is where these trees originated. They thrive in warm conditions in sandy soil and can be identified by their long, grey-green twisted needles.

This species of black pine has been a mainstay of commercial plantations, where it is valued for its straight habit and quick rate of growth. However, in recent years Corsican pines have been struck by a disease called red band needle blight, caused by a fungus which thrives in our increasingly warm climate.

ABOUT PINES

Pine trees are evergreens and have leaves in the form of needles. These grow in groups of two (as on this Corsican pine), three or five with a sheath holding them together at their base.

Pine needles are prickly and the cones hang downwards, tucked in close to the branches. The bark becomes thick and scaly as the trees age.

CROSSBILLS

Eating anything looks hard with this beak, but it is perfect for prising open pine cones to reach the seeds inside. Crossbills are born with straight bills which cross as they start to mature.

FACTFILE

HABITAT: Plantations, scrub and sand dunes

SIZE: Up to 60 m

FLOWERS: May to June

HABIT: Tall, straight with an open crown

TYPE: Evergreen

BURNS: Well but spits

FACTFILE
HABITAT: Woodland
edges and hedgerows
SIZE: Up to 10 m
FLOWERS: Apr to May
HABIT: Messy round
shape, dense branches
TYPE: Deciduous
BURNS: Well, scented

CRAB APPLE
Malus sylvestris

THE WORD CRAB in its name is said to be due to the crabby or spiny appearance of this fruit tree, and its older branches do bear thorns. The crab apple is a member of the rose family which is most evident at blossom-time, when the delicate pink rose-like flowers are on display. The wood, like the blossom, has a pink tinge and is good for making decorative objects.

Malus sylvestris means "forest apple" yet it is not a tree of deep forests, for it needs light to grow and prefers solitary sites where its yellow-green apples can ripen in the sun.

LICHEN

You may see crab apple trees with a crusty covering of an organism called lichen living over their gnarled grey bark. There are many types of lichen, and most grow only in unpolluted areas, so it is usually a sign of good air quality.

WILDLIFE

Most trees deliver some benefit to wildlife but the crab apple is in a league of its own. The wonderfully scented flowers provide pollen and nectar to foraging insects, especially bees and bumblebees; caterpillars of many butterfly and moth species happily gorge on the leaves; while the fruit is greedily devoured by mammals such as foxes and deer as well as lots of different birds.

To human taste, crab apples are much more tart than cultivated apples but they do make an excellent jelly.

FRUIT GALLERY

BEING A FLOWER ON A TREE is all about getting pollinated. Once this has been achieved, it is time to turn into a fruit. Being a fruit is all about protecting the seed or seeds inside and then helping them leave home. You may think of fruit as succulent foods but this gallery displays some of their other varied forms.

QUINCE

MEDLAR

FIG

ROWAN

ELDER

WILD CHERRY

BLACKTHORN

SPINDLE

MULBERRY

HORSE CHESTNUT

BEECH

LONDON PLANE

WALNUT

PEDUNCULATE OAK

HAZEL

ASH

SYCAMORE

WYCH ELM

BLACK LOCUST

INDIAN BEAN TREE

HORNBEAM

43

CRACK WILLOW
Salix fragilis

SNAP! THAT IS THE SOUND the branches of the crack willow make when they break off. They are particularly brittle where they join the trunk, hence the *fragilis* (fragile) part of this tree's scientific name. Many crack willows are pollarded, so you may not see the tree looking as large or as majestic as this one.

Bits of broken crack willow that float downstream are quick to establish themselves as new trees, and soon corridors of crack willow may line a river. In some countries, such as Australia, this ability to spread has led to its being seen as an invasive species.

WILDLIFE

Many insects depend on this tree – such as the red underwing moth, whose caterpillars feed on the leaves. Crack willow helps to stabilise riverbanks, but if the canopy becomes too thick it can affect the wildlife living below.

FLOWERS AND LEAVES

Some tree species have male and female flowers on the same tree but those of the crack willow exist on separate trees. The male flowers are a showy yellow colour, and insects make a beeline for these first before pollinating the smaller green female ones (shown below). Crack willow is easy to confuse with white willow but its leaves are longer and a more glossy green.

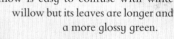

FACTFILE
HABITAT: Wet soil,
mostly river valleys
SIZE: Up to 25 m
FLOWERS: Apr to May
HABIT: Rounded,
often multi-trunked
TYPE: Deciduous
BURNS: Well when dry

DOGWOOD
Cornus sanguinea

THE SCIENTIFIC NAME of a plant is given in Latin, with the family name listed first – in this case *cornus* meaning horny – followed by the part of the name that distinguishes the particular species. Here, *sanguinea* means blood-red – the colour of the young shoots and also of the leaves in autumn.

Blood is also a good way to remember one use of dogwood which was for arrows for killing people or animals. In 1991, the mummified body of a man who lived over 3,000 years ago was found in the Alps along with arrows made from dogwood.

A CLOSER LOOK

The tiny white flowers of the dogwood tree appear in hedgerows in June, which is surprisingly late compared with many other trees. Though the smell is not always agreeable to humans, the clusters of small white dogwood flowers attract early summer insects; the leaves are grazed on by animals and are eaten by caterpillars such as those of the casebearer moth; and the black berries are enjoyed in the autumn by birds.

SHOOTS

You are very likely to notice dogwood on a walk or drive through the countryside in winter. This is when the claret-red stems of the young shoots are on full display – a burst of colour in an otherwise faded world.

FACTFILE

HABITAT: Hedgerows,
scrub, woodland edges
SIZE: Up to 4 m
FLOWERS: June
HABIT: Bushy, untidy
shrublike tree
TYPE: Deciduous
BURNS: Well

DOUGLAS FIR

Pseudotsuga menziesii

THE FIRST DOUGLAS FIR was brought to Europe from North America by the Scottish botanist David Douglas in 1827. With the subsequent rise of commercial forestry, plantations of this fast-growing conifer sprang up for use in building and for paper.

Legend has it that a mouse sought refuge from a forest fire by climbing inside the cone of a Douglas fir. Like all good legends it has some truth behind it, for this tree is relatively resistant to fire and the cones have three bracts sticking out of one end, which bear some resemblance to a mouse's back legs and tail.

WILDLIFE

Red squirrels and pine martens make their homes in Douglas fir trees while birds of prey, such as this common buzzard, build their nests in them.

BARK

Like skin, bark wrinkles over time. Some trees stay youthfully smooth for many years, such as the beech. However, the Douglas fir ages quickly, changing from an even grey to a deeply furrowed purple-brown.

FOLIAGE

Key features that help to identify a Douglas fir tree include: needles encircling the branches and which leave scars when pulled away; brown, scaly buds; and cones hanging down.

FACTFILE
HABITAT: Lowland forests, parks, gardens
SIZE: Up to 60 m
FLOWERS: Mar to May
HABIT: Narrow with few lower branches
TYPE: Evergreen
BURNS: Poorly

CONES

TREES BEARING CONES are called conifers.
That may not surprise you, but here are
some facts you may not know:

•

There are both male and female cones.
Male cones are often smaller and found
lower down a tree at the base of a branch,
with female cones located higher up and
at the branch tip.

•

Male cones produce fine grains of pollen
to be released on the wind in the hope
of finding female cones to land on. Once
fertilised by pollen, female cones produce
seeds. The scales on the cones harden,
protecting the seeds inside until they ripen.

•

Mature cones stay closed in cold, wet
weather and open on warm, dry days.

•

Many people eat pine nuts – these are
seeds from inside the cones of stone pines.

FACTFILE
HABITAT: Hedgerows, woods, gardens
SIZE: Up to 10 m
FLOWERS: May to June
HABIT: Wayward arching branches
TYPE: Deciduous
BURNS: Poorly

ELDER

Sambucus nigra

THERE IS A SAYING that summer begins when elder is in flower and ends when the berries are ripe. With climate change, it is increasingly difficult to tell when seasons begin and end, but as elderflowers can still be seen in June and the berries ripen in September, this saying seems reasonably reliable.

Elder is a fast-growing plant which, given enough space and light, will grow into a small tree. Seen by some as invasive, it happily regenerates if cut back by sending up vigorous shoots, and is quick to populate otherwise abandoned areas.

WILDLIFE

Elder often grows near warrens because the rabbit droppings help to fertilise the soil. Elder flowers, leaves and berries are also a food source for many insects, birds and mammals.

CORDIAL, WINE AND WITCHES

The flowers and fruit of the elder tree make delicious cordials, jams, jellies and wines, and the buds are held to be a good substitute for capers when pickled. These culinary uses are strange given that most parts of the tree – including the leaves, seeds, bark and flowers – all contain traces of poison in their raw state and so require careful preparation.

The Romans valued the juice from the berries for making hair dye and the wood for warding off witches.

FACTFILE
HABITAT: Forests and
large gardens
SIZE: Up to 50 m
FLOWERS: Mar to May
HABIT: Tapering trunk,
drooping branches
TYPE: Deciduous conifer
BURNS: Poorly, spits

EUROPEAN LARCH
Larix decidua

TREES CREATE DIFFERENT atmospheres around them, and there is something particularly peaceful and uplifting about the larch. In the spring, it puts forth early, vibrantly green needles which by autumn will fade to a soothing burnished gold. When the leaves finally fall to the ground, they create a carpet of needles which muffles the sound of footsteps.

It is only one of a few conifer species to shed its leaves in winter. This lets light through beneath the trees, making it possible for woodland flowers such as bluebells to grow up in spring.

WOOD USES AND BARK

The tall, straight trunks rise up quickly and can be harvested within 40 years, by which time the bark is red-brown and deeply cracked. Larch timber is strong and uses include fencing, railway sleepers and planks for boat-building.

FLOWERS AND NEEDLES

Larch rose is the name sometimes given to the striking red female flower which slowly hardens to form a small, egg-shaped cone. The cones may stay on the tree for many years and they make identifying larch easier. Look out for the needles arranged in tufts on the branches, too.

WOODLAND WILDLIFE

TREES PROVIDE WILDLIFE with food and places to shelter, nest or roost throughout the year. Woodlands seem most alive in the spring when birds are in full song and many animals are beginning to emerge from their winter sleep. This is the time for making nests and finding possible partners.

Wildlife-rich trees are usually those that have been in a region for the longest time and have populated it most abundantly. In the United Kingdom, these include oaks, willows, hawthorns and birches, with oaks alone home to at least 250 types of insect.

There can be more life in a dead tree than in a living one. Dead wood provides vital microhabitats on which almost half of all woodland wildlife species depend.

EUROPEAN SILVER FIR
Abies alba

THIS FIR, NATIVE to the mountains of central Europe, prefers cool, wet climates and thrives best in stands of mixed trees. The silver in the name refers to the trunk and not to the foliage, though the underside of each needle has two white bands. Characteristically, silver firs are often seen with broken lower branches, as here.

This is the original Christmas tree, popular in many parts of Europe. The needles usually stay on the tree for up to 12 years – though not when brought inside and adorned with decorations! In the right location, this tree can live for up to 600 years.

FOREST FOES

Seeing large animals in the wild can be thrilling. However, deer such as this red stag are a real problem, for they eat their way through forest understory vegetation. particularly savouring silver-fir seedlings.

ABOUT FIRS

To work out whether you are looking at a fir, a spruce or a pine, look to see if the needles are inserted into the twig singly or in groups. If singly, then it is likely to be a fir or a spruce. Next, try rolling the needle. If you can do this easily, then it is probably a spruce, but if it is flat and hard to roll, the chances are it is a fir.

European silver-fir needles are long with notches in the ends of them. The cones grow upwards on the branches (unlike on the Douglas fir) and take 18 months to ripen.

FACTFILE
HABITAT: Damp, shady
uplands in any soil
SIZE: Up to 50 m
FLOWERS: Apr to May
HABIT: Conical or
with flattened top
TYPE: Evergreen
BURNS: Well

FIELD MAPLE

Acer campestre

THIS IS OUR ONLY NATIVE maple. It is a small tree which can withstand being cut back, making it a popular choice for hedgerows. It is also found along woodland edges, where it seeks out light with its lobed leaves. The branches are unusual in that they often become ridged like the corky bark of the trunk.

Field-maple sap is not as sweet as that from other maple species but it is still used by some to sweeten food. It is drained from the trunk in early spring when the sap is moving up the tree. The wood is used for firewood and charcoal, and for making bowls.

LEAVES, FLOWERS AND FRUIT

The leaves are arranged in pairs and are recognisable by their five rounded lobes. If you look closely, you will see that they are hairy on both sides and that the leaf stalk exudes a milky sap when cut.

The small, lemony coloured flowers develop into winged keys, ripening in late September before being carried away on the wind.

THROUGH THE SEASONS

In the spring, bright green field-maple leaves emerge which have a pinkish tinge. The green slowly deepens and the leaves thicken as the year progresses. By autumn, the green disappears leaving a fine display of yellows.

FACTFILE
HABITAT: Hedgerows, gardens, woodlands • SIZE: Up to 25 m
FLOWERS: Apr to May • HABIT: Dense, round crown
TYPE: Deciduous • BURNS: Well

AUTUMN COLOURS

As THE DAYS GET SHORTER and winter approaches, nature puts on one of her best seasonal shows: her autumn-leaf spectacular. Some years, the reds, yellows, and oranges of the leaves seem to be particularly vibrant which is largely because of warm days, cool nights and not too much rainfall. But why do leaves change colour at all?

Deciduous trees shut down over the cold, dark, winter months. Their leaves have spent the year collecting energy from the sun and converting it into food in a process called photosynthesis. A key ingredient in this chemical reaction is a green pigment called chlorophyll, which gradually stops being produced in the autumn as light levels decline. This allows the other pigments contained within leaves to show through, until eventually the leaves fall.

HAWTHORN
Crataegus monogyna

FEW TREES LIGHT UP the countryside quite as much as the hawthorn with its clusters of white blossom which adorn our hedgerows in May. Like the blackthorn which flowers in March, the hawthorn belongs to the rose family and makes an excellent hedgerow plant with its sharp, densely packed thorny branches.

Hawthorn blossom, or May blossom as it is often called, has a heavy, sweet scent, especially on sunny days. One chemical the flowers produce is the same as that released by decomposing bodies, so there is a good reason if you find it unappealing.

WILDLIFE

In the spring, insects clamber over the blossom in search of nectar, pollinating the flowers as they go. Birds, such as the greenfinch (below), yellowhammer and song thrush, feed on the colourful berries.

HAWS AND LEAVES

The bright red colour of the berries stands out against the brilliant green of the hawthorn's lobed leaves. The fruit are known as haws and each one bears a single seed. To make the best jam or jelly, the berries should be sufficiently ripe and chosen from younger trees.

The leaves are red when they first open but soon fade to pink and then green, though it is hard to see the leaves until the blossom has disappeared.

FACTFILE
HABITAT: Hedgerows,
gardens, wood edges
SIZE: Up to 15 m
FLOWERS: May
HABIT: Dense mass
with round head
TYPE: Deciduous
BURNS: Well, slowly

HEDGEROWS

HAWTHORN, HAZEL, holly and hornbeam – these are just some of the trees that are found in our hedgerows. What makes them ideally suited for this is that they can all tolerate harsh weather conditions and being cut back, and most have a dense network of branches which makes passage through them difficult. Apart from their use as natural barriers, hedgerows form vital wildlife corridors where numerous animals including birds, spiders, butterflies, moths, mice and hedgehogs can live and move from place to place in relative safety.

While the value to wildlife is incalculable, what can be estimated is the age of a hedge. This is worked out by counting the number of species in a 10-metre stretch and multiplying it by a hundred years. So three species would mean, roughly, a 300-year-old hedge.

FACTFILE
HABITAT: Woods, hedgerows, scrubland
SIZE: Up to 12 m
FLOWERS: Jan to Mar
HABIT: Shrublike and multi-stemmed
TYPE: Deciduous
BURNS: Well

HAZEL
Corylus avellana

MANY TREES ARE MORE IMPOSING than the bushlike hazel, yet few can have been as valuable to humans. Hazel groves used to be planted throughout the countryside in order to harvest both the nuts and the wood. The trees would then be coppiced (cut back) to stimulate new growth, though hazel will send up new shoots whether coppiced or not.

As today, the nuts were valued as a source of protein and the bendy stems made excellent hurdles for fences; the basis for walls when combined with clay; as well as baskets and tools.

FLOWERS AND FRUIT

The sight of hazel catkins in late January is one of the first signs that winter is ending. These yellow male flowers, commonly called lambs' tails, open and expand before releasing their pollen on the wind. Turn the page to see one in action. The tiny crimson threads of the female flowers (below) wait to receive the pollen, after which clusters of up to four nuts will form.

WILDLIFE

Hazelnuts are loved by (some) humans and also by dormice, deer and squirrels. Squirrels tend to split the nuts in half while dormice make round holes in the side.

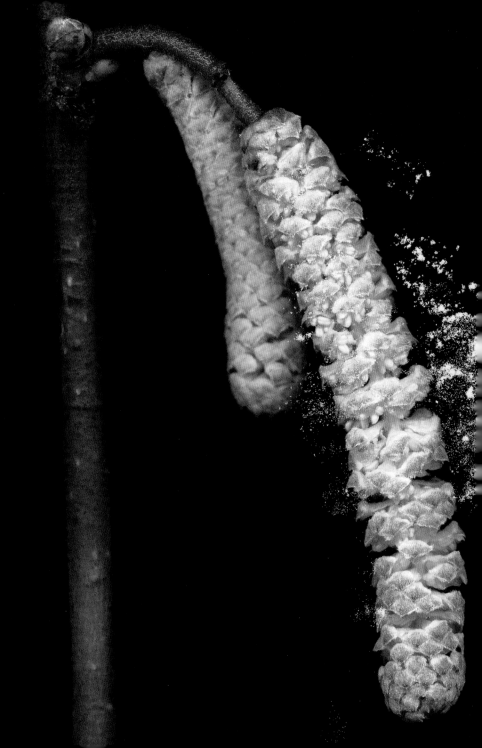

CATKINS

EVEN IN THE DEPTHS of winter, you may see the pale male yellow catkins of the hazel tree hanging down from its otherwise bare branches. Catkins are clusters of tiny flowers – these hazel ones have about 240 each – which slowly lengthen and open to release pollen.

Hazel, willow, walnut and sweet chestnut are just some of the tree species that bear catkins. Their drooping form makes them perfectly suited to wind pollination, though some receive help from insects as well. Here you can clearly see the pollen grains ready to be carried away on the wind to fertilise the hazel's female flowers.

HOLLY
Ilex aquifolium

WITH SPIKY LEAVES and bright red berries, the holly tree is instantly recognisable. If you look closely at this silhouette, you will see that the leaves on the higher branches are not as prickly as the ones lower down. This is probably because they are safely beyond the reach of grazing animals.

The thick glossy leaves stay on the tree for several years and, when they do fall, it takes time for them to rot. This allows few plants or fungi to grow beneath and instead offers shelter to hibernating animals such as mammals, reptiles and amphibians.

FLOWERS AND FRUIT

The tiny white flowers of the holly tree are about as inconspicuous as the fruit is obvious and they grow close to the branch. Trees are either male or female, which is why not every tree produces berries – though holly that grows under larger trees tends not to fruit either.

There are many superstitions linking holly with evil spirits and ill fortune. The only sure thing is that if you eat the berries or leaves, you will be sick.

HOLLY BLUE

Spring sees this small butterfly lay its eggs at the base of the holly's flower buds. Two weeks later, tiny caterpillars hatch out and hungrily devour the surrounding leaves and flowers. Holly blues lay more eggs in the autumn, but these are laid on ivy.

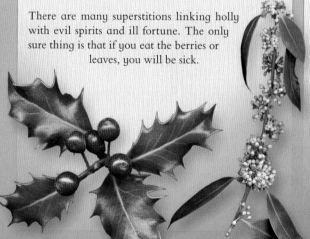

FACTFILE

HABITAT: Woods, hedgerows, gardens • SIZE: Up to 20 m
FLOWERS: May to June • HABIT: Spire-shaped if left to grow
TYPE: Evergreen • BURNS: Well and quickly

FACTFILE

HABITAT: Woods, hedgerows, parks • SIZE: Up to 30 m
FLOWERS: Apr • HABIT: Wide crown, profuse branches
TYPE: Deciduous • BURNS: Well and slowly

HORNBEAM
Carpinus betulus

THE HORNBEAM PERFORMS on many levels – it puts forth the most radiant autumn colours, has distinctive flowers and fruit and is a haven for wildlife. Yet, for some reason, it falls under the "tree radar" and many would have a hard time recognising one.

The timber from hornbeam is white and dense and it would definitely not be the tree to practise on if you were new to woodwork, for it is extremely tough. This makes it the perfect choice for things that need to withstand a constant hammering such as chopping blocks, piano keys and flooring.

FLOWERS

These dangling male catkins appear at the same time as the leaves, in April. The female catkins wait for the wind to carry the pollen to them before ripening to form pairs of nutlets in winged, papery cases.

A CLOSER LOOK

The picture of hornbeam bark below shows the silvery pattern of a reasonably young tree. Hornbeams can live for up to 300 years, and over time the vertical lines you can see develop into deeply etched grooves.

Hornbeam and beech trees are easy to confuse, especially as both keep their leaves during the winter. However, hornbeam leaves have distinct ridges on them and serrated edges, which beech leaves lack.

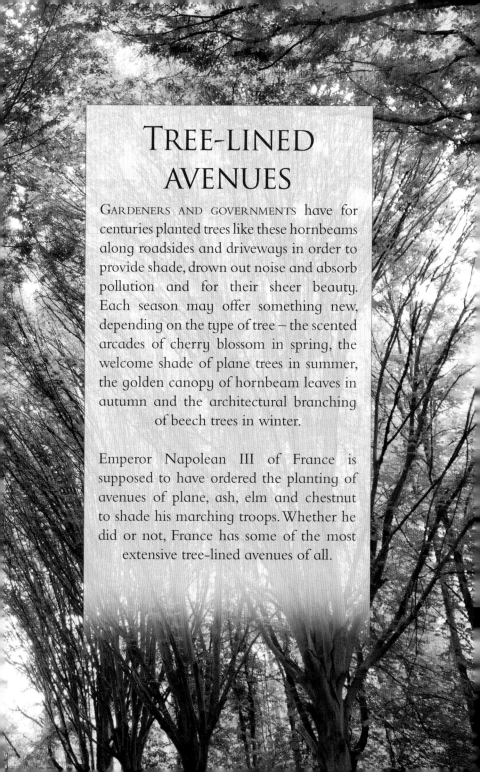

TREE-LINED AVENUES

GARDENERS AND GOVERNMENTS have for centuries planted trees like these hornbeams along roadsides and driveways in order to provide shade, drown out noise and absorb pollution and for their sheer beauty. Each season may offer something new, depending on the type of tree – the scented arcades of cherry blossom in spring, the welcome shade of plane trees in summer, the golden canopy of hornbeam leaves in autumn and the architectural branching of beech trees in winter.

Emperor Napolean III of France is supposed to have ordered the planting of avenues of plane, ash, elm and chestnut to shade his marching troops. Whether he did or not, France has some of the most extensive tree-lined avenues of all.

FACTFILE
HABITAT: Parks, gardens, roadsides • SIZE: Up to 40 m
FLOWERS: May • HABIT: Tall with an oval crown
TYPE: Deciduous • BURNS: Poorly, spits

HORSE CHESTNUT
Aesculus hippocastanum

IF YOU RELY ON INSECTS for pollination, you first need to attract them. Few trees do this more dramatically than the horse chestnut with its tall columns of fragrant flowers. Markings on the petals change from yellow to pink once the flowers have been pollinated, signalling to bees not to visit.

The reason for the *hippo*, or horse, part of the name is unclear. It may arise from the use of conkers for horse medicines, or else perhaps from the horseshoe-shaped scar left by the leaves when they fall – which you can just see at the base of the twig below.

INVADERS

Horse-chestnut wood decays easily, and large boughs often break off. The resulting open wounds encourage the growth of fungi, such as chicken-of-the-woods (below). Pests such as the leaf miner moth may also attack the tree, causing leaves to discolour and fall early.

A CLOSER LOOK

Every part of this tree is distinctive, making it one of the easiest trees to identify. The leaves are broad and hand-like with five or seven leaflets joined at a central point; the buds are large and sticky; the flowers are blousy and fragrant; and, as if all this wasn't enough, the spiky fruit cases split open to reveal glossy fruits, perfect for playing conker games.

POLLINATION

THIS BUMBLEBEE IS BUSILY gathering nectar from the flowers of the sycamore tree. Nectar is the sugary prize that trees use to entice insects to visit them. As the insects forage, they pick up tiny grains of pollen from male flower parts and transfer them to female ones, allowing fertilisation to take place and seeds to be produced.

The sycamore is pollinated by both the wind and insects. You can usually guess which method trees favour by looking at and sniffing the flowers – if the flowers have that "look at me" air about them, with large petals and a strong fragrance, they are likely to be insect pollinated. If they lack petals and have hanging flower clusters which are easily blown around, then they are probably wind pollinated.

FACTFILE
HABITAT: Heaths, open
woods, rocky outcrops
SIZE: Up to 10 m
FLOWERS: May
HABIT: Very variable
as bush or tree
TYPE: Evergreen
BURNS: Slowly, well

JUNIPER
Juniperus communis

HOW DO YOU KNOW if you are looking at a juniper tree? The easiest way to tell is by examining its needles. They are arranged in threes around the twigs, and are sharp and fragrant with a white band on their upper side. The berry-like cones are green at first. These turn blue once they mature but, as this takes up to three years, both colours may be seen at the same time.

Juniper is found far and wide throughout North America, Europe and Asia. It is remarkably tolerant of harsh weather conditions and poor soil, as long as there is enough light.

THE MANY USES OF JUNIPER
How many trees do you know of that have healing powers? Willow bark is famed for its painkilling properties but juniper deserves to be equally well known, for oils taken from all parts of the tree have formed the basis for remedies for centuries.

If you crush a ripe juniper berry it releases a wonderful aroma, making it a popular addition to drinks as well as flavouring for use in food dishes.

WILDLIFE
When winter grips the land and the ground is frozen, juniper berries sustain hungry birds such as thrushes. Deer and rabbits graze on the foliage too, despite the sharp needles.

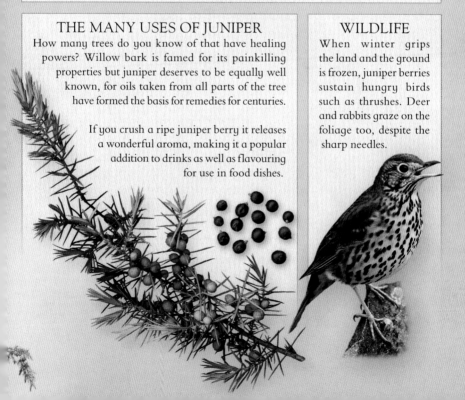

LIME, COMMON
Tilia x europaea

AVENUES OF COMMON lime trees line many of the streets in our towns and cities. Even though it is one of our tallest broadleaf trees, it manages to thrive in these urban conditions because it can withstand heavy pruning as well as air pollution.

This is not the tree that bears the lime fruit. It is a cross (known as a hybrid) between the small-leaved lime and the large-leaved lime. It can be hard to tell them apart as they all have heart-shaped leaves, but the trunk of the common lime is more ridged and knobbly and often has shoots growing up from its base.

FLOWERS AND FRUIT

It takes 40 years for these trees to produce flowers, and when they do, the fragrance is intense and sweet. Clusters of creamy-yellow flowers bloom in July attracting hordes of insects, especially bees, which produce a wonderful honey from the nectar.

Once the lime flowers have been pollinated, they set to form small, round fruit which hang down waiting to be carried away on the wind.

WILDLIFE

This ladybird is laying its eggs on a lime leaf. When the eggs hatch, the larvae will feed on tiny insects called aphids. These aphids release a sticky substance which covers anything lying underneath them (other leaves, cars, the pavement), which then get covered in dirt.

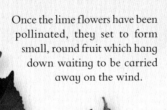

FACTFILE
HABITAT: Parks, gardens, roadsides • SIZE: Up to 45 m
FLOWERS: July • HABIT: Tall and pyramid-shaped
TYPE: Deciduous • BURNS: Poorly

THE FOREST FLOOR

"And into the forest I go, to lose my mind and find my soul" – JOHN MUIR, NATURALIST

BROADLEAF FORESTS ARE made of up of trees that lose their leaves in winter. The reason more flowers can be seen in this type of woodland during the spring, compared with any other time of year, is that they benefit from the warming effect of the sun and its bright light. Both of these provide ideal conditions for woodland flowers.

Plants that take full advantage of the brighter conditions early in the spring include primroses, wood anemones, snowdrops and lesser celandines, not to mention bluebells like these. Once the leaves on the trees open, the forest becomes a shady place where fewer flowers thrive.

FACTFILE

HABITAT: Roadsides, parks and field edges
SIZE: Up to 36 m
FLOWERS: Apr to May
HABIT: Straight and fast-growing
TYPE: Deciduous
BURNS: Quickly

LOMBARDY POPLAR

Populus nigra "Italica"

THE LOMBARDY POPLAR'S RISING spire-like shape can make one feel very small. This eye-catching tree reaches an impressive height within just a few years, which has made it a popular choice for farmers and gardeners for use in a field boundary, or as a screen or windbreak.

What grows quickly upwards also does so downwards, and the roots of poplar trees can be a menace as they stretch far and wide looking for any available water. However, the lifespan of most Lombardy poplars is short, as they are prone to disease.

TAKING A CLOSER LOOK

In winter, the Lombardy poplar's sharp and pointed golden buds sit alternately on the gnarled twigs. You can see the red male catkins below, which emerge in March before the small, triangular leaves.

BRANCHES

Most trees have large boughs from which smaller branches grow. The Lombardy poplar is different. A mass of long branches curves upwards close to the trunk, giving the tree its distinctive narrow, upright shape.

WILDLIFE

Birds such as magpies nest in its branches, while the larvae of some butterflies and moths, such as this rare Camberwell beauty, lay their eggs on the leaves. The hungry caterpillars then devour them on hatching.

LONDON PLANE
Platanus x hispanica

THIS LARGE TREE may seem unsuited to city life but quite the opposite is true. It can shed off flakes of bark when the trunk gets too dirt-laden – a particularly useful skill in a polluted urban atmosphere. This is what gives this tree its mottled appearance, with the older darker bark peeling off to reveal the creamy new trunk underneath. The London plane is also extremely sturdy, can grow in any type of soil and withstand being cut back.

This tree is a hybrid – a cross between the Oriental plane and the American plane – and is not found in the wild.

LEAVES
Kicking up fallen plane leaves in autumn can be very satisfying although not for those who have to clear them up. They are variable in size, and before falling turn from green to yellow.

FRUIT
Green spiky fruit form from the pollinated flowers and slowly darken to brown. These stay on the tree through winter, until the spring sees them burst open to release the seeds inside.

LACEWOOD
The flecked patterns of London plane timber are valued by woodworkers who use them to decorate furniture and for carvings. Wood with this type of marking is known as lacewood.

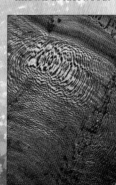

FACTFILE

HABITAT: Roadsides,
parks, large gardens

SIZE: Up to 44 m

FLOWERS: May

HABIT: Straight trunk,
high bending boughs

TYPE: Deciduous

BURNS: Well, if dry

BARK GALLERY

BARK IS THE OUTER LAYER of a tree's stem and branches. An inner part, called the phloem, carries water and minerals from the roots up to the leaves, and sap made by the leaves downwards. Bark also protects a tree from weather, animals and diseases. As it ages, it often becomes more wrinkled and changes colour.

| ASH | ASPEN | BEECH |

| BLACK POPLAR | BOX | CRACK WILLOW |

| DOUGLAS FIR | FIELD MAPLE | HAWTHORN |

HOLLY

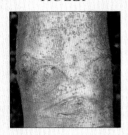

HORSE CHESTNUT

JUNIPER

LOMBARDY POPLAR

LONDON PLANE

PEDUNCULATE OAK

SCOTS PINE

SILVER BIRCH

SWEET CHESTNUT

SYCAMORE

WALNUT

YEW

NORWAY SPRUCE
Picea abies

WITH EVENLY SPACED branches rising up to form a pyramid, this is a popular Christmas tree. It thrives in mountainous regions where it can withstand bitterly cold conditions, but struggles in the heat, as its shallow roots find it hard to reach water reserves.

Though many are grown to be sold as Christmas trees each year, the Norway spruce is an important source of timber. Its creamy-white colour gives it the name whitewood and it has a variety of uses, from telegraph poles, building supports and pulp for paper to soundboards for musical instruments.

WILDLIFE

Tawny owls and other birds of prey roost in the branches; squirrels feed on the cones; and wild boar and deer gnaw away the bark, as do many insects.

ABOUT SPRUCES

Spruce-tree needles grow out singly from the branches and at the base of each one there is a tiny peg. This comes away if you pull a needle off the tree, but will remain when the needle falls off naturally. Spruce trees also have cones, which hang down, and papery bark.

Below on the left are the Norway spruce's yellow male flowers and on the right is a crimson female one. Once fertilised, the female flower turns down and ripens to become a brown, cigar-shaped cone.

FACTFILE
HABITAT: Plantations,
woods, mountainsides
SIZE: Up to 50 m
FLOWERS: May to June
HABIT: Tall and thin
with pointed crown
TYPE: Evergreen
BURNS: Poorly

FACTFILE
HABITAT: Woods,
parks, gardens, fields
SIZE: Up to 40 m
FLOWERS: Apr to May
HABIT: Large trunk,
spreading crown
TYPE: Deciduous
BURNS: Slowly and well

PEDUNCULATE OAK

Quercus robur

ALSO KNOWN AS the English or common oak, this mighty tree grows wide, tall and deep and may live for over a thousand years. It was once a sacred tree around which people would worship, and for centuries the fine timber has been valued for making houses, boats and furniture as well as for fuel and charcoal.

Oak trees are often twisted and gnarled and are commonly seen with broken branches or hollowed-out insides. Many other trees would die if damaged like this, but the oak contains chemicals to ward off potential invaders such as insects, fungi and diseases.

LEAVES

A peduncle is a stalk, which is what the acorns of this oak tree have. The leaves, however, are stalkless unlike those of the sessile oak.

WILDLIFE

A single oak tree will provide shelter, food and a place to nest and roost for hundreds of animal species in its lifetime. The acorns are a key food source especially for mammals such as deer, squirrels and mice and for birds such as the jay. Insects feed on every part of the tree and they, in turn, become meals for reptiles, birds and amphibians.

Below is a picture of an oak gall. The larvae of a wasp cause the tree to produce growths like these, but they rarely do the oak any harm.

FROM SEED TO TREE

AN OAK CAN LIVE for over 1,000 years and produce 10 million acorns in its lifetime. So why aren't we overrun with oak trees? Well, the likelihood is that only a few will ever reach maturity.

What makes it so difficult? When it falls to the ground, an acorn has to escape being eaten by hungry animals, such as squirrels. It then needs enough oxygen, and water at the right temperature, in order to start to send out roots and shoots. The shoots make tasty morsels for yet more hungry animals and, if the young tree survives that, it has to avoid being cut down by humans, or struck down by diseases or bad weather. On top of that, it needs sufficient space and light in which to grow – not easy to find in a forest.

This is not just the story of the oak tree – it is the story of almost every tree.

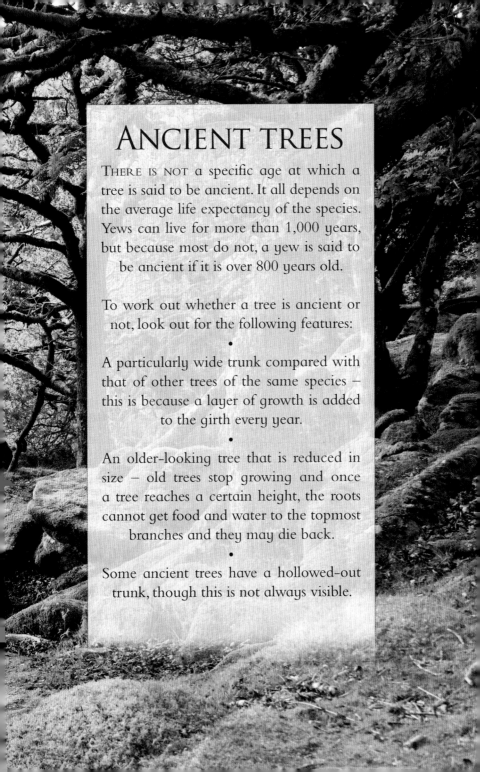

ANCIENT TREES

THERE IS NOT a specific age at which a tree is said to be ancient. It all depends on the average life expectancy of the species. Yews can live for more than 1,000 years, but because most do not, a yew is said to be ancient if it is over 800 years old.

To work out whether a tree is ancient or not, look out for the following features:

•

A particularly wide trunk compared with that of other trees of the same species – this is because a layer of growth is added to the girth every year.

•

An older-looking tree that is reduced in size – old trees stop growing and once a tree reaches a certain height, the roots cannot get food and water to the topmost branches and they may die back.

•

Some ancient trees have a hollowed-out trunk, though this is not always visible.

ROWAN
Sorbus aucuparia

EVERYTHING ABOUT THIS TREE is pretty and delicate and yet it is most at home on high, rocky hillsides where it can withstand severe frosts. It is also known as the mountain ash, for this reason and because its leaves are similar to those of the common ash. Elsewhere, its slender form makes it a popular ornamental tree in parks and gardens and along the sides of city streets.

There is a long history of rowan trees being thought to provide protection against evil spirits – look out for them near churches – and cutting down a rowan was believed to bring bad luck.

WILDLIFE
What bird could resist clusters of bright berries? They are a favourite of waxwings, thrushes and blackbirds, especially during the harsh winter months. Deer find the young shoots delicious and beavers gnaw on the branches.

BERRIES
The berries ripen to a vivid orangy-red colour in the autumn. They are rich in vitamin C and can be used to make a rather tart rowanberry jelly. Cutting a berry in half will reveal that it is like a mini apple.

FOLKLORE
There are many theories about the type of winter that lies ahead based on the number and colour of rowan berries in the autumn. As beliefs in different countries vary, it is safer to listen to the long-range weather forecast.

FACTFILE
HABITAT: Parks, gardens, hillsides • SIZE: Up to 20 m
FLOWERS: Apr to May • HABIT: Small, neat delicate tree
TYPE: Deciduous • BURNS: Excellently

FACTFILE

HABITAT: Mountains, heaths, coasts, parks
SIZE: Up to 40 m
FLOWERS: Apr to May
HABIT: Tall, often with rounded crown
TYPE: Evergreen
BURNS: Hot and fast

SCOTS PINE
Pinus sylvestris

SOME TREES ARE perfectly balanced with branches growing evenly all around. What is noticeable about the Scots pine is its irregular shape and habit of losing its lower branches. Look out also for the orange-pink bark of its upper trunk which gradually becomes greyer and more broken towards the ground.

Scotland's national tree is home to many creatures, from red squirrels and pine martens to crested tits and capercaillies. It is a common forestry tree because it grows quickly and straight, and is harvested for use in the paper and construction industries.

FUNGI

Some fungi live in harmony with trees, such as this fly agaric, which grows in the soil beneath Scots pines and silver birch trees in particular. Other types of fungi attack and seriously weaken or even kill these trees.

LEAVES AND CONES

All pine trees have needles arranged in groups. Those of the Scots pine grow in pairs and are slightly twisted. They are also shorter than those of some other pines and have a distinctive blue-green colour.

In May, the male flowers release clouds of yellow pollen (below right). Once fertilised by this pollen, the female flowers turn into green and then brown pointed cones which take two years to ripen. The scales on these cones have a distinctive bump in the centre of them.

SESSILE OAK
Quercus petraea

LOOKING UPWARDS, you can see the branches of the sessile oak tree fanning outwards from its straight, furrowed trunk. Though the tree provides shade, light still gets through, allowing other plants to grow beneath it. This oak species has particularly deep roots, which means that it can tolerate dry, often rocky situations compared with the more damp-loving pedunculate oak.

Below ground, the roots spread at least twice as far as the crown, and woven between them are miles of fungi helping the tree to connect with other trees and find water and nutrients.

WILDLIFE

Oaks are among the most important trees for wildlife, especially invertebrates such as this stag beetle. This insect's larvae feed on rotten wood, spending up to five years underground before emerging as adults.

LEAVES, FLOWERS AND FRUIT

The deep green leaves of the sessile oak have long stalks compared with those of the pedunculate oak, yet its acorns have none and are attached directly to the branch. Sessile means stalkless and it is this feature of its acorns that gives the tree its name.

The yellow male catkins hang from the tree in May waiting for the wind to carry their pollen to the small female flowers. It is from these pollinated flowers that the acorn fruit will form.

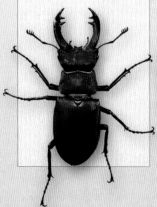

FACTFILE

HABITAT: Woods, parks, large gardens • SIZE: Up to 40 m
FLOWERS: May • HABIT: Broad crown, long straight trunk
TYPE: Deciduous • BURNS: Slowly and well when dry

FACTFILE
HABITAT: Woods, heaths, gardens • SIZE: Grows to 30 m
FLOWERS: Apr to May • HABIT: Straight and fast-growing
TYPE: Deciduous • BURNS: Quickly

SILVER BIRCH
Betula pendula

THIS IS AN EASY TREE to identify with its striking papery-white, graceful trunk that sways in the breeze. Look out for the small triangular leaves with their jagged edges, as well as the male flowers (hanging golden catkins) and female ones (short and green) which appear on the same tree from April to May.

Silver birch trees are the chancers of the forest world. The tiny seeds are carried by the wind and then often find a new patch of ground in which to germinate. They grow quickly when young, and perhaps that is why they have quite short lives.

USES

The leaves were once used as a type of tea as well as being food for cattle. Before the use of parchment and paper, the bark served as a material for writing on. Today, the light wood is used for making furniture and toys.

BIRCH TREES AND WILDLIFE

Siskins, redpolls and greenfinches feed on birch seeds, while woodpeckers often nest in the trunk. Below the light airy canopy, bluebells, violets and anemones flower and fungi such as fly agaric and chanterelles thrive. Birch is home to many insects, attracting aphids and hungry ladybirds, as well as angle shades and buff-tip moths.

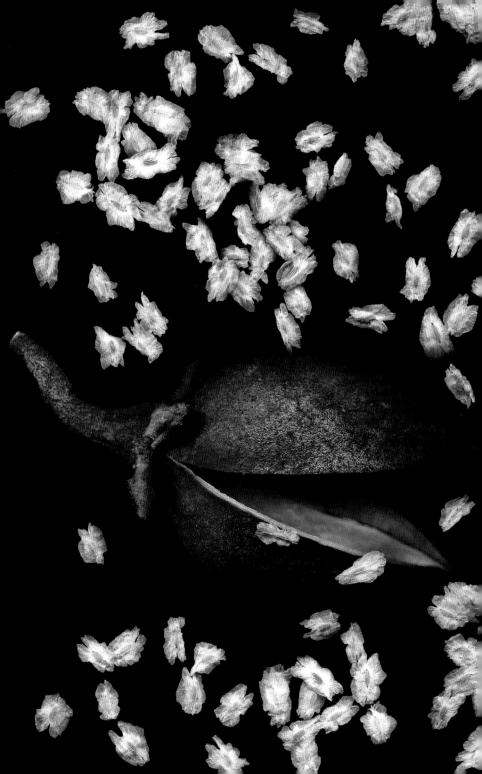

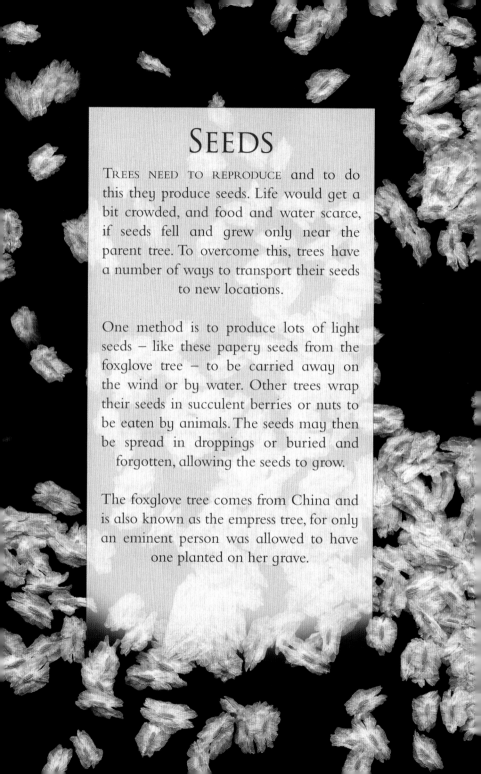

SEEDS

TREES NEED TO REPRODUCE and to do this they produce seeds. Life would get a bit crowded, and food and water scarce, if seeds fell and grew only near the parent tree. To overcome this, trees have a number of ways to transport their seeds to new locations.

One method is to produce lots of light seeds – like these papery seeds from the foxglove tree – to be carried away on the wind or by water. Other trees wrap their seeds in succulent berries or nuts to be eaten by animals. The seeds may then be spread in droppings or buried and forgotten, allowing the seeds to grow.

The foxglove tree comes from China and is also known as the empress tree, for only an eminent person was allowed to have one planted on her grave.

SWEET CHESTNUT
Castanea sativa

THIS IS ONE of the easiest trees to identify: its glossy green leaves are long and pointed with jagged edges; the trunk is deeply furrowed and twisted in older trees; and the reddish-brown nuts are carried in spiky green husks.

It is believed that this tree was first brought to Britain by the Romans and it has been valued for its wood and its fruit ever since. The seeds (chestnuts) can be roasted and eaten whole or as a paste, or ground to a flour to make bread. The wood is hard-wearing and commonly used for fencing and building work.

WILDLIFE

Sweet chestnut groves are a key habitat for many insects, including this heath fritillary butterfly as well as over 200 species of moth. Wildlife thrive on all parts of the tree with the nuts being an especially vital winter food source.

FLOWERS AND FRUIT

The male flowers of the sweet chestnut look like exploding fireworks thanks to their yellow colour, their length and the sparkling stamens on the individual flowers. They bloom late compared with those of other trees and produce a strong scent to attract insects.

Once the job of pollination is done, the male withers and dies while the female flower starts to develop into the familiar glossy brown nut. Nut numbers vary from year to year and are larger where light and warmth are available.

FACTFILE

HABITAT: Mixed woodland, large gardens • SIZE: Up to 35 m
FLOWERS: June to July • HABIT: Broad crown, twisted trunk
TYPE: Deciduous • BURNS: Well, but spits

FACTFILE
HABITAT: Woods, hedgerows, parks • SIZE: Up to 35 m
FLOWERS: May • HABIT: Sturdy trunk and large domed crown
TYPE: Deciduous • BURNS: With moderate heat when dry

SYCAMORE

Acer pseudoplatanus

THESE SYCAMORE LEAVES look fresh and green, and yet by late summer they are likely to be covered with black spots. These are caused by the relatively harmless tar-spot fungus. Sycamore trees in cities do not suffer the same fate, as the fungus that creates the marks cannot tolerate polluted air.

This fast-growing tree can live for several hundred years, but in a working woodland it is usually cut for timber when it reaches the age of 70. The wood is pale, strong and valued for making furniture, flooring, utensils and musical instruments.

LEAVES AND SEEDS

In every season, the sycamore has some distinctive characteristic. In winter, the pinky-brown twigs have thick, green, scaly buds. In spring and summer, the lobed leaves emerge and grow with striking red stems. In autumn, the tree's famous winged "helicopter" seeds, known as samara, spin to the ground.

HOVERFLIES

Watch out for hoverflies sunbathing on sunlit sycamore leaves in the spring. Hoverflies prey on the tiny green aphid insects that feed on sycamore leaves in May. Where there is a healthy supply of tasty insects like these, there will also be small birds to feed on them.

ALL YEAR ROUND

As THE SEASONS CHANGE through the year, so too do deciduous trees – ones that lose their leaves – like the maple opposite.

SPRING
The days lengthen and warm, causing sap to rise up inside the maple's trunk carrying food and water to the branches. The leaves and flowers start to emerge and the process of reproduction begins.

SUMMER
The bright green of the young leaves darkens as the tree grows in the sunlight and warmth. Its flowers are pollinated by insects and wind, causing fruit to form.

AUTUMN
The tree's winged fruit ripen and are carried on the wind. The days shorten and cool and the maple's sap falls, causing the leaves to change colour and drop.

WINTER
Now the tree stands bare, waiting for warmer air and the longer days of spring.

FACTFILE
HABITAT: Hedgerows, fields, gardens
SIZE: Up to 30 m
FLOWERS: Apr to May
HABIT: Large, upward-spreading branches
TYPE: Deciduous
BURNS: Fragrant, well

WALNUT

Juglans regia

HOW DO YOU KNOW you are looking at a walnut tree? Walnut trees like space and light and so tend to grow singly or in small groups in fields. The upward-reaching branches bear fresh pale green leaves, while the trunk is surprisingly slender compared with the tree's broad crown. The bark is smooth and silvery grey in young trees and becomes grooved with age.

Try crushing walnut leaves to see what smell is released. Some say it is like shoe polish while others say it calls to mind citrus fruit. Be careful of the juice as it can stain the hands black.

FLOWERS

The striking, thick male catkins (below) appear on the tree in May before the leaves. The wind spreads their golden pollen on to the female flowers which grow on the same tree.

WALNUT USES

In October, the thick green husk of the ripened fruit splits open to release the gnarled brown walnut inside. Walnuts are an excellent food source – not only are they delicious; they are rich in oil, vitamins and minerals.

Walnut trees are prized for their wood which is worked to make fine furniture. Extracts from the bark and leaves also serve as the basis for many medicines.

WHITEBEAM
Sorbus aria

THE WHITEBEAM IS ONE of those satisfying trees that is easy to identify even from a distance. The undersides of the leaves are strikingly white and it is these that catch the eye, as well as the tree's upward-reaching branches. Look out, too, for the clusters of white flowers in spring and the orangy-red berries of autumn.

Whitebeam timber is hard and although it is not widely used today, it was once valued for making tools, cogs and furniture. Nowadays, whitebeam is a popular ornamental tree and is regularly planted in parks and streets.

WILDLIFE
Hungry birds such as woodpigeons, crows and thrushes feast on the berries in autumn. These are too large for smaller birds, which pick at the fruit instead. The whitebeam seeds are then spread in the birds' droppings.

LEAVES
When the leaves emerge, they are lined above and below with white hairs. These protect the young leaves from the sun and give the tree a strikingly white appearance. As the leaves age, only the lower sides stay hairy.

BERRIES
Some years are better than others in terms of berry numbers; no matter how many the tree produces, they are always quick to shrivel once ripe. Historically, the berry flesh was added to flour to make bread, and all parts of the tree were used to feed livestock.

FACTFILE

HABITAT: Hedgerows, woods, cities, scrub • SIZE: Up to 15 m
FLOWERS: May • HABIT: Small tree with oval or round crown
TYPE: Deciduous • BURNS: Too valuable to be burned

TREE GROWTH

IF YOU LOOK AT THIS cross-section of a tree, you will see that it is made up of rings. Each one marks a year of growth – wide rings form when conditions are good; narrow rings indicate the opposite. But what causes these rings to form?

During spring and summer, the tree grows fast and puts down large cells, but during autumn and winter, growth slows and only small cells are produced. It is these small cells – which are closely packed together – that appear as dark rings or bands. The older wood, which forms the core of the tree, is known as heartwood.

To age a tree that has been cut down or died, count the number of rings you can see. One ring equals a year's growth. If you see alternate darker and lighter circles, count each pair together as one year.

FACTFILE
HABITAT: Riverbanks, marshland • SIZE: Up to 30 m
FLOWERS: Apr to May • HABIT: Often leaning, branches grow
upwards • TYPE: Deciduous • BURNS: Poorly, and sparks

WHITE WILLOW
Salix alba

ON SUNNY DAYS IN THE SPRING, bees seek out the nectar from white willow flowers. The male flowers hang in clusters forming long, golden catkins (shown below) while the shorter greeny-white female ones grow on separate trees. Willows like damp, light conditions such as along canals and riverbanks where the roots help to keep the banks stable.

The white part of this tree's name comes from the silky pale undersides of its narrow leaves, which can be seen most easily when the wind blows through them.

USES

The painkiller aspirin comes from an active ingredient found in the bark of young white willows. Some people chew the bark itself as a cure for pain. Withies – long, flexible willow shoots – are perfect for making baskets, too.

OTHER WILLOW SPECIES

It can be tricky trying to identify the many different types of willow. One popular variety is the weeping willow, which you can see below. This hybrid arrived from the East and is a familiar sight by the side of ponds on village greens.

The wood of all willows is particularly light and quite soft, and one type of white willow – known as the cricket-bat willow – is tough and elastic. It has the ability to withstand being struck with force, which makes it perfect for the construction of cricket bats.

125

WILD CHERRY
Prunus avium

CLUSTERS OF FRAGRANT FLOWERS cover this tree in late April just after the leaves appear. The wild cherry tree here is in full bloom, which may last only a week or two depending on the weather. Its bark is particularly striking thanks to its shiny reddish-brown colour and horizontal lines. If damaged, the tree oozes a gum-like substance which helps to seal and protect the wound.

The golden wood of this species is one of the most valuable timbers in Europe and is used to make fine furniture, flooring, doors and musical instruments.

WILDLIFE
You need to be quick if you want to gather the cherries, as birds such as starlings and thrushes will strip the trees bare in a twinkling. Badgers, foxes and other mammals then gorge on any leftovers.

FRUIT
Once pollinated, the flowers form cherries which ripen quickly, turning from green to red, then almost black. Few other fruit trees have crops that are ready to pick as early in the year as June.

LEAVES
The large oval leaves have jagged edges and long stalks. In late summer, when the tree shuts down in preparation for winter, they change from green to wonderful shades of yellow, orange and red. The leaves are poisonous to livestock if they eat too many.

FACTFILE
HABITAT: Hedgerows,
woodland edges
SIZE: Up to 30 m
FLOWERS: Apr to May
HABIT: Short, straight
trunk, round crown
TYPE: Deciduous
BURNS: Well, slowly

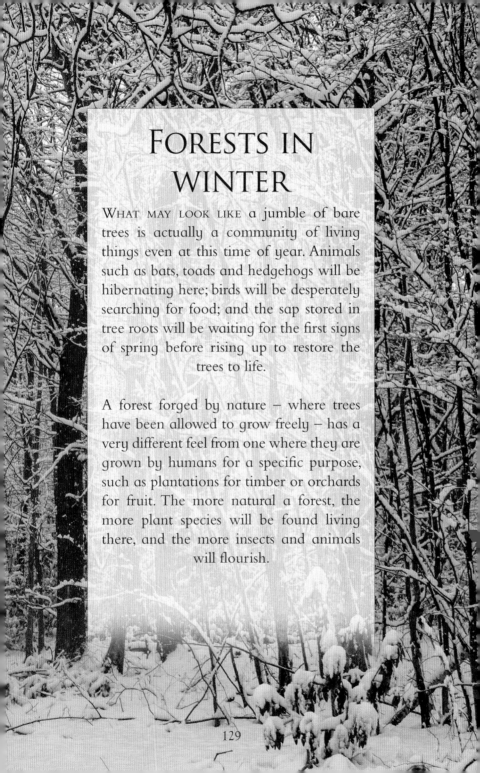

FORESTS IN WINTER

WHAT MAY LOOK LIKE a jumble of bare trees is actually a community of living things even at this time of year. Animals such as bats, toads and hedgehogs will be hibernating here; birds will be desperately searching for food; and the sap stored in tree roots will be waiting for the first signs of spring before rising up to restore the trees to life.

A forest forged by nature – where trees have been allowed to grow freely – has a very different feel from one where they are grown by humans for a specific purpose, such as plantations for timber or orchards for fruit. The more natural a forest, the more plant species will be found living there, and the more insects and animals will flourish.

FACTFILE
HABITAT: Woods, hedges and parks • SIZE: Up to 30 m
FLOWERS: Feb to Mar • HABIT: Broad, round crown
TYPE: Deciduous • BURNS: Liable to smoke

WYCH ELM
Ulmus glabra

WYCH IS AN OLD ENGLISH word meaning bendy and, historically, the wood was shaped to form wheels and water pipes. The wood is also extremely hard and can tolerate being submerged in water, and was traditionally used to make boats, sea barriers, coffins, chairs and mallets.

Look for this striking tree in damp woods and along hedgerows and streams. Along with the leaves and seeds shown below, you might recognise the wych elm by its clusters of dark red flowers in early spring or perhaps by its yellow autumn display.

DISEASE

About 25 million mature trees – mostly English elms but some wych elms – died in Britain in the 1970s as a result of Dutch elm disease. This was caused by a fungus and spread on the mouth parts of wood-boring beetles, leaving trails like the ones below.

A CLOSER LOOK

The leaves and seeds are what really help to identify a wych elm. With virtually no stalks, the ribbed leaves feel rough and end unevenly at their base. The tip either tapers to a point or else has three distinctive prongs.

Each elm seed is encased in a papery disc, light enough to be carried away on the wind. The seeds ripen in May on trees that are at least 30 years old.

FACTFILE

HABITAT: Churchyards, woods, hedges

SIZE: Up to 25 m

FLOWERS: Feb to Mar

HABIT: Dense foliage, often many trunks

TYPE: Evergreen

BURNS: Fierce heat

YEW
Taxus baccata

THE DENSE, DARK, SPREADING FORM of the yew haunts the churchyards of Britain. Its ability to live for hundreds if not thousands of years, and regenerate if damaged, has enhanced its sacred status. Unlike most trees, it thrives in the shady world of the forest understory and tolerates all but waterlogged sites.

An ancient 400,000-year-old yew spearhead, known as the Clacton Spear, is proof of the saying that a post made of yew will outlive one of iron. More recently, yew wood was favoured for making furniture and another lethal weapon – the longbow.

FLOWERS

Yews have the most unflowery flowers. The female ones are green and look like tiny buds, while the male ones (shown below) are small and pale yellow. Clouds of pollen released by the male flowers can cause allergic reactions such as headaches and tiredness.

POISONOUS PARTS

All parts of the yew are poisonous except for the one thing that looks as though it should be – the red fleshy cup surrounding the seed. This is called an aril and is actually a type of cone. Birds feast on these safely as the poisonous seed inside passes through them undigested. Yew leaves are highly toxic, especially if crushed or dried, and can be fatal to horses and cows, though not to deer. Many yews have been felled because of the danger they pose to livestock; they are now protected.

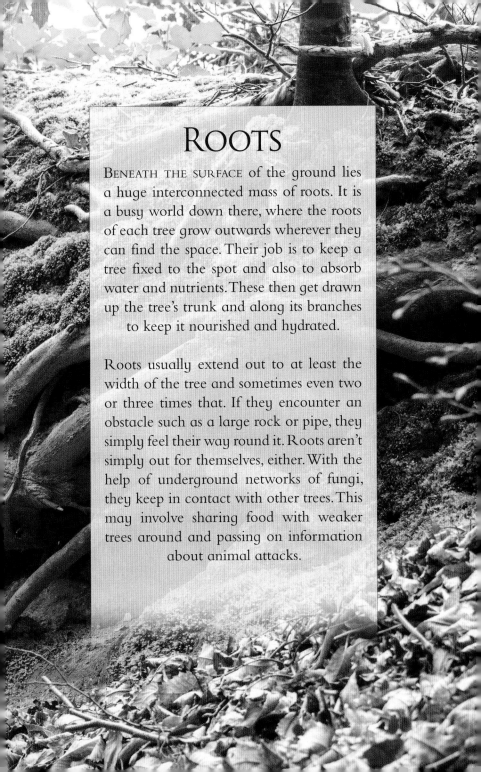

ROOTS

BENEATH THE SURFACE of the ground lies a huge interconnected mass of roots. It is a busy world down there, where the roots of each tree grow outwards wherever they can find the space. Their job is to keep a tree fixed to the spot and also to absorb water and nutrients. These then get drawn up the tree's trunk and along its branches to keep it nourished and hydrated.

Roots usually extend out to at least the width of the tree and sometimes even two or three times that. If they encounter an obstacle such as a large rock or pipe, they simply feel their way round it. Roots aren't simply out for themselves, either. With the help of underground networks of fungi, they keep in contact with other trees. This may involve sharing food with weaker trees around and passing on information about animal attacks.

WOODLAND PLANTS

THE LIFE OF A WOODLAND is constantly changing. Each season heralds new plants which grow, reproduce and die. Most flowers, though, appear in the springtime before the leaves have fully opened overhead. This is just a small selection of the most common plants you may encounter on a woodland walk.

BLUEBELL

BRACKEN

BRAMBLE

BUGLE

COMMON VIOLET

DOG ROSE

EARLY PURPLE ORCHID

FOXGLOVE

HONEYSUCKLE

IVY

LESSER CELANDINE

LILY OF THE VALLEY

MALE FERN

MISTLETOE

PRIMROSE

SNOWDROP

SMALL BALSAM

STINGING NETTLE

WILD GARLIC

WOOD ANEMONE

WOOD AVENS

GLOSSARY

ANCIENT TREE
A mature tree that is old compared with other trees of the same species.

ARIL
An extra covering around a seed, such as the red fleshy cup surrounding a yew seed.

BARK
The outer protective layer of a tree. It often cracks or peels as the tree grows.

BLOSSOM
A term used for attractive flowers, especially those of fruit trees such as wild cherry and crab apple.

BOTANIST
The term used to describe a scientist or enthusiast who studies plants.

BRACT
A leaf-like structure at the base of a flower or between the scales of a cone.

BROADLEAF TREE
A tree with thin, flat leaves of varying shapes and sizes.

CANOPY
The upper leafy layer of trees.

CATKIN
A hanging cluster of flowers, often long, produced by certain tree families such as hazel, walnut, willow and birch.

CHLOROPHYLL
A green substance found in plants which helps to convert energy from sunlight into food.

COMPOUND LEAF
A leaf divided into smaller leaflets, like those of an ash or a walnut.

CONE
The fruit of a conifer, usually made up of tough overlapping scales which protect the seeds inside.

CONIFER
A tree with needle-like or scaly leaves that produces its seeds inside woody cones.

CROWN
The part of a tree above the ground, made up of the branches and leaves.

COPPICING
Cutting back a tree to ground level to encourage it to grow new shoots.

DECIDUOUS TREE
A tree that loses its leaves in winter.

EVERGREEN TREE
A tree that keeps its leaves all year round.

FOLIAGE
The leaves of a plant.

FOREST
A large area covered with trees that is bigger than a woodland.

GERMINATE
To start growing.

GROVE
A small group of trees.

HABIT
The general appearance of a plant such as upright, branching or compact.

HARDY
A plant that can survive difficult conditions such as cold weather.

HUSK
The outer casing surrounding some fruit or seeds such as walnuts.

HYBRID
A cross between two different species.

INVASIVE SPECIES
A tree (or any living organism) that has been introduced to a new location and causes harm.

LACEWOOD
The name used to describe the patterned wood of some trees including the London plane.

LEAFLET
One of several leaf-like parts making up a compound leaf.

LOBED LEAF
A leaf shaped with large indentations but not divided into separate leaflets.

LEAF MARGIN
The edge of a leaf.

MAST
The seeds of forest trees such as beech and oak trees.

NATIVE TREE
A tree that has existed in a place for a long time and was not introduced by humans.

NECTAR
A sweet liquid produced by insect-pollinated flowers.

NODE
The place on a stem where a flower or leaf emerges.

NUTRIENTS
Energy-giving substances taken in by plants and animals.

ORNAMENTAL TREE
A tree grown for decoration rather than for its wood or fruit.

PEDUNCLE
The stalk of a flower or fruit.

PHOTOSYNTHESIS
The process by which plants use light, water and gases to make food.

PLANTATION
Large numbers of trees planted together for wood production or other forest crops.

POLLARDING
Cutting a trunk high up so that it produces new branches which animals cannot reach.

POLLEN
Fine grains produced by male flowers in order to fertilise female ones.

POLLINATION
Transferring pollen from male to female flowers so that seeds can form.

PRUNING
Trimming or cutting back a plant such as a tree in order to control growth.

RESIN
A sticky substance that oozes out of some trees, such as pines, when the trunk is damaged.

ROOT
The part of a plant that fixes it below ground and seeks out water and minerals.

SAMARA
A dry fruit where the seed is housed inside a papery case which helps carry the seed away from the tree.

SAP
The energy-giving liquid flowing through plants, made up of water, sugars and minerals.

SESSILE
Attached directly to a branch, without a stalk, such as the acorns of the sessile oak.

SHRUB
A woody plant with many stems, smaller than a tree.

SIMPLE LEAF
A leaf made up of one undivided surface, though its edges may be wavy or jagged.

SPECIES
A group of organisms, such as plants and animals, that share the same characteristics and can reproduce with one another.

SUCKER
A shoot that grows up from the base of a tree.

TIMBER
The wood from a tree used by people to make things.

TREE
A plant producing woody growth, larger than a shrub.

UNDERSTORY
An area of a woodland that is beneath the canopy of trees.

WOODLAND
An area covered with trees, smaller than a forest.

INDEX

"The true meaning of life is to plant trees, under whose shade you do not expect to sit."
NELSON HENDERSON, FARMER

Acknowledgements

WITH THANKS TO
Sunita Gahir – Prepress designer
Yolanta Motylinska – Production adviser
Penny Phillips – Proof reader
Kate Inskip – Indexer

PICTURE CREDITS
Key: b = below; l = left; c = centre; r = right
23 Michel Gunther/Biosphoto/Diomedia; **27bl** Ian Redding/
shutterstock.com; **34bl** (cone) Kazakov Maksim/shutterstock.
com; **34br** Mr R. Graz/shutterstock.com; **38br** Robert
L. Kothenbeutel/shutterstock.com; **40** Ken Leslie/Alamy;
44bl Vitalii Hulai/shutterstock.com; **45** imageBROKER/
Alamy; **58bc** Universal Images Group North America LLC/
DeAgostini/Alamy; **59** Danier/shutterstock.com; **69br** Richard
Peterson/shutterstock.com; **90br** Coconee/ shutterstock.com;
106bc (acorn) Mircea Costina/shutterstock.com; **107** Hervé
Lenain/Alamy; **124** John Martin/Alamy; **130** Avalon/Photoshot
License/Alamy.

All other images © Fine Feather Press